THE MENACE OF THE RELIGIOUS MOVIE

By

A. W. Tozer

pastor, preacher, author, magazine editor, spiritual mentor

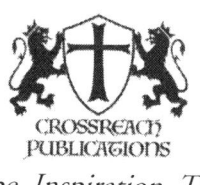

Hope. Inspiration. Trust.

<u>We're Social! Follow Us for New Titles and Deals:</u>
FaceBook.com/CrossReachPublications
@CrossReachPub

Available In Paperback And eBook Editions
Please go online For More Great Titles
Available Through CrossReach Publications.
And If You Enjoyed This Book Please Consider Leaving A
<u>Review On Amazon</u>. That Helps Us Out A Lot. Thanks.

© 2017 <u>CrossReach Publications</u>
All Rights Reserved, Including The Right To Reproduce
This Book Or Portions Thereof In Any Form Whatever.

INTRODUCTION

When God gave to Moses the blueprint of the Tabernacle He was careful to include every detail; then, lest Moses should get the notion that he could improve on the original plan, God warned him solemnly, "And look that thou make them after their pattern, which was shown thee in the mount." God, not Moses, was the architect. To decide the plan was the prerogative of the Deity. No one dare alter it so much as a hairbreadth.

The New Testament Church also is built after a pattern. Not the doctrines only but the methods are divinely given. The doctrines are expressly stated in so many words. Some of the methods followed by the early New Testament Church had been given by direct command; others were used by God's specific approval, having obviously been commanded the apostles by the Spirit. The point is that when the New Testament canon was closed the blueprint for the age was complete. God has added nothing since that time.

From God's revealed plan we depart at our peril. Every departure has two consequences, the immediate and the remote. The immediate touches the individual and those close to him;

the remote extends into the future to unknown times, and may expand so far as to influence for evil the whole Church of God on earth.

The temptation to introduce "new" things into the work of God has always been too strong for some people to resist. The Church has suffered untold injury at the hands of well-intentioned but misguided persons who have felt that they know more about running God's work than Christ and His apostles did. A solid train of box cars would not suffice to haul away the religious truck which has been brought into the service of the Church with the hope of improving on the original pattern. These things have been, one and all, positive hindrances to the progress of the Truth, and have so altered the divinely-planned structure that the apostles, were they to return to earth today, would scarcely recognize the misshapen thing which has resulted.

Our Lord while on earth cleansed the Temple, and periodic cleansings have been necessary in the Church of God throughout the centuries. Every generation is sure to have its ambitious amateur to come up with some shiny gadget which he proceeds to urge upon the priests before the altar. That the Scriptures do not justify its existence does not seem to bother him at all. It is brought in anyway and presented in the very name of Orthodoxy. Soon it is identified in the minds of the Christian public with all that is good and holy. Then, of course, to attack the gadget is to attack the Truth itself. This is an old familiar technique so often and so long practiced by the devotees of error that I marvel how the children of God can be taken in by it.

We of the evangelical faith are in the rather awkward position of criticizing Roman Catholicism for its weight of unscriptural impedimenta and at the same time tolerating in our own churches a world of religious fribble as bad as holy water or the elevated host. Heresy of method may be as deadly as heresy of message. Old-line Protestantism has long ago been smothered to death by extra-scriptural rubbish. Unless we of the gospel churches wake up soon we shall most surely die by the same means.

Within the last few years a new method has been invented for imparting spiritual knowledge; or, to be more accurate, it is not new at all, but is an adaptation of a gadget of some years standing, one which by its origin and background belongs not to the Church but to the world. Some within the fold of the Church have thrown their mantle over it, have "blessed it with a text" and are now trying to show that it is the very gift of God for our day. But, however eloquent the sales talk, it is an unauthorized addition nevertheless, and was never a part of the pattern shown us on the mount.

I refer, of course, to the religious movie.

For the motion picture as such I have no irrational allergy. It is a mechanical invention merely and is in its essence amoral; that is, it is neither good nor bad, but neutral. With any physical object or any creature lacking the power of choice it could not be otherwise. Whether such an object is useful or harmful depends altogether upon who uses it and what he uses it for. No moral quality attaches where there is no free choice. Sin and righteousness lie in the will. The motion picture is in the same class as the automobile, the typewriter, or the radio: a powerful instrument for good or evil, depending upon how it is applied.

For teaching the facts of physical science the motion picture has been useful. The public schools have used it successfully to teach health habits to children. The army employed it to speed up instruction during the war. That it has been of real service within its limited field is freely acknowledged here.

Over against this is the fact that the motion picture in evil hands has been a source of moral corruption to millions. No one who values his reputation as a responsible adult will deny that the sex movie and the crime movie have done untold injury to the lives of countless young people in our generation. The harm lies not in the instrument itself, but in the evil will of those who use it for their own selfish ends.

I am convinced that the modern religious movie is an example of the harmful misuse of a neutral instrument. There are sound reasons for my belief. I am prepared to state them.

That I may be as clear as possible, let me explain what I do and do not mean by the religious movie. I do not mean the missionary picture nor the travel picture which aims to focus attention upon one or another section of the world's great harvest field. These do not come under consideration here.

By the religious movie I mean that type of motion picture which attempts to treat spiritual themes by dramatic representation. These are (as their advocates dare not deny) frank imitations of the authentic Hollywood variety, but the truth requires me to say that they are infinitely below their models, being mostly awkward, amateurish and, from an artistic standpoint, hopelessly and piteously bad.

These pictures are produced by acting a religious story before the camera. Take for example the famous and beautiful story of the Prodigal Son. This would be made into a movie by treating the narrative as a scenario. Stage scenery would be set up, actors would take the roles of Father, Prodigal Son, Elder Brother, etc. There would be plot, sequence and dramatic denouement as in the ordinary tear jerker shown at the Bijou movie house on Main Street in any one of a thousand American towns. The story would be acted out, photographed, run onto reels and shipped around the country to be shown for a few wherever desired.

The "service" where such a movie would be shown might seem much like any other service until time for the message from the Word of God. Then the lights would be put out and the picture turned on. The "message" would consist of this movie. What followed the picture would, of course, vary with the circumstances, but often an invitation song is sung and a tender appeal is made for erring sinners to return to God.

Now, what is wrong with all this? Why should any man object to this or go out of his way to oppose its use in the house of God? Here is my answer:

1. IT VIOLATES THE SCRIPTURAL LAW OF HEARING.

The power of speech is a noble gift of God. In his ability to open his mouth and by means of words make his fellows know what is going on inside his mind, a man shares one of the prerogatives of the Creator. In its ability to understand the spoken word the human mind rises unique above all the lower creation. The gift which enables a man to translate abstract ideas into sounds is a badge of his honor as made in the image of God.

Written or printed words are sound symbols and are translated by the mind into hearing. Hieroglyphics and ideograms were, in effect, not pictures but letters, and the letters were agreed-upon marks which stood for agreed-upon ideas. Thus words, whether spoken or written, are a medium for the communication of ideas. This is basic in human nature and stems from our divine origin.

It is significant that when God gave to mankind His great redemptive revelation He couched it in words. "And God spake all these words" very well sums up the Bible's own account of how it got here. "Thus saith the Lord" is the constant refrain of the prophets. "The words that I speak unto you, they are spirit, and they are life," said our Lord to His hearers. Again He said, "He that heareth my word, and believeth on him that sent me, hath everlasting life." Paul made words and faith to be inseparable: "Faith cometh by hearing, and hearing by the word of God." And he also said, "How shall they hear without a preacher?" (Romans 10:14)

Surely it requires no genius to see that the Bible rules out pictures and dramatics as media for bringing faith and life to the human soul.

The plain fact is that no vital spiritual truth can be expressed by a picture. Actually all any picture can do is to recall to mind some truth already learned through the familiar medium of the spoken or written word. Religious instruction and words are bound together by a living cord and cannot be separated without fatal loss. The Spirit Himself, teaching soundlessly within the heart, makes use of ideas previously received into the mind by means of words.

If I am reminded that modern religious movies are "sound" pictures, making use of the human voice to augment the dramatic action, the answer is easy. Just as far as the movie depends upon spoken words it makes pictures unnecessary; the picture is the very thing that differentiates between the movie and the sermon. The movie addresses its message primarily to the eye, and the ear only incidentally. Were the message addressed to the ear as in the Scriptures, the picture would have no meaning and could be omitted without loss to the intended effect. Words can say all that God intends them to say, and this they can do without the aid of pictures.

According to one popular theory the mind receives through the eye five times as much information as the ear. As far as the external shell of physical facts is concerned this may hold good, but when we come to spiritual truth we are in another world entirely. In that world the outer eye is not too important. God addresses His message to the hearing ear. "We look," says Paul, "not at the things which are seen, but at the things which are not seen: for the things which are seen are temporal; but the things which are not seen are eternal" (2 Corinthians 4:18). This agrees with the whole burden of the Bible, which teaches us that we should withdraw our eyes from beholding visible things, and fasten the eyes of our hearts upon God while we reverently listen to His uttered words.

"The word is nigh thee, even in thy mouth, and in thy heart: that is, the word of faith, which we preach" (Romans 10:8). Here, and not somewhere else, is the New Testament pattern, and no human being, and no angel from heaven has any right to alter that pattern.

2. The religious movie embodies the mischievous notion that religion is, or can be made, a form of entertainment.

This notion has come upon us lately like a tidal wave and is either openly taught or tacitly assumed by increasing numbers of people. Since it is inextricably bound up with the subject under discussion I had better say more about it.

The idea that religion should be entertaining has made some radical changes in the evangelical picture within this generation. It has given us not only the "gospel" movie but a new type of religious journalism as well. It has created a new kind of magazine for church people, which can be read from cover to cover without effort, without thought--and without profit. It has also brought a veritable flood of religious fiction with plastic heroines and bloodless heroes like no one who has ever lived upon this well-known terrestrial ball.

That religion and amusement are forever opposed to each other by their very essential natures is apparently not known to this new school of religious entertainers. Their effort to slip up on the reader and administer a quick shot of saving truth while his mind is on something else is not only futile, it is, in fact, not too far short of being plain dishonest. The hope that they can convert a man while he is occupied with the doings of some imaginary hero reminds one of the story of the Catholic missionary who used to sneak up on sick people and children and splash a little holy water on them to guarantee their passage to the city of gold.

I believe that most responsible religious teachers will agree that any effort to teach spiritual truth through entertainment is at best futile and at worst positively injurious to the soul. But entertainment pays off, and the economic consideration is always a powerful one in deciding what shall and what shall not be offered to the public--even in the churches.

Deep spiritual experiences come only from much study, earnest prayer and long meditation. It is true that men by thinking cannot find God; it is also true that men cannot know God very well without a lot of reverent thinking. Religious movies, by appealing directly to the shallowest stratum of our minds, cannot but create bad mental habits which unfit the soul for the reception of genuine spiritual impressions.

Religious movies are mistakenly thought by some people to be blessed of the Lord because many come away from them with moist eyes. If this is a proof of God's blessing, then we might as well go the whole way and assert that every show that brings tears is of God. Those who attend the theater know how often the audiences are moved to tears by the joys and sorrows of the highly paid entertainers who kiss and emote and murder and die for the purpose of exciting the spectators to a high pitch of emotional excitement. Men and women who are dedicated to sin and appointed to death may nevertheless weep in sympathy for the painted actors and be not one bit the better for it. The emotions have had a beautiful time, but the will is left untouched. The religious movie is sure to draw together a goodly number of persons who cannot distinguish the twinges of vicarious sympathy from the true operations of the Holy Ghost.

3. The Religious Movie is a Menace to True Religion Because it Embodies Acting, a Violation of Sincerity.

Without doubt the most precious thing any man possesses is his individuated being; that by which he is himself and not someone else; that which cannot be finally voided by the man himself nor shared with another. Each one of us, however humble our place in the social scheme, is unique in creation. Each is a new whole man possessing his own separate "I-ness" which makes him forever something apart, an individual human being. It is this quality of uniqueness which permits a man to enjoy every reward of virtue and makes him responsible for every sin. It is his selfness, which will persist forever, and which distinguishes him from every creature which has been or ever will be created.

Because man is such a being as this all moral teachers, and especially Christ and His apostles, make sincerity to be basic in the good life. The word, as the New Testament uses it, refers to the practice of holding fine pottery up to the sun to test it for purity. In the white light of the sun all foreign substances were instantly exposed. So the test of sincerity is basic in human character. The sincere man is one in whom is found nothing foreign; he is all of one piece; he has preserved his individuality unviolated.

Sincerity for each man means staying in character with himself. Christ's controversy with the Pharisees centered around their incurable habit of moral play acting. The Pharisee constantly pretended to be what he was not. He attempted to vacate his own "I-ness" and appear in that of another and better man. He assumed a false character and played it for effect. Christ said he was a hypocrite.

It is more than an etymological accident that the word "hypocrite" comes from the stage. It means actor. With that instinct for fitness which usually marks word origins, it has been used to signify one who has violated his sincerity and is playing a false part. An actor is one who assumes a character other than his own and plays it for effect. The more fully he can become possessed by another personality the better he is as an actor.

Bacon has said something to the effect that there are some professions of such nature that the more skillfully a man can work at them the worse man he is. That perfectly describes the profession of acting. Stepping out of our own character for any reason is always dangerous, and may be fatal to the soul. However innocent his intentions, a man who assumes a false character has betrayed his own soul and has deeply injured something sacred within him.

No one who has been in the presence of the Most Holy One, who has felt how high is the solemn privilege of bearing His image, will ever again consent to play a part or to trifle with that most sacred thing, his own deep sincere heart. He will thereafter be constrained to be no one but himself, to preserve reverently the sincerity of his own soul.

In order to produce a religious movie someone must, for the time, disguise his individuality and simulate that of another. His actions must be judged fraudulent, and those who watch them with approval share in the fraud. To pretend to pray, to simulate godly sorrow, to play at worship before the camera for effect--how utterly shocking to the reverent heart! How can Christians who approve this gross pretense ever understand the value of sincerity as taught by our Lord? What will be the end of a generation of Christians fed on such a diet of deception disguised as the faith of our fathers?

The plea that all this must be good because it is done for the glory of God is a gossamer-thin bit of rationalizing which should not fool anyone above the mental age of six. Such an argument parallels the evil rule of expediency which holds the end is everything, and sanctifies the means, however evil, if only the end be commendable. The wise student of history will recognize this immoral doctrine. The Spirit-led Church will have no part of it.

It is not uncommon to find around the theater human flotsam and jetsam washed up by the years, men and women who have played false parts so long that the power to be sincere has forever gone from them. They are doomed to everlasting duplicity. Every act of their lives is faked, every smile is false, every tone of their voice artificial. The curse does not come causeless. It is not by chance that the actor's profession has been notoriously dissolute. Hollywood and Broadway are two sources of corruption which may yet turn America into a Sodom and lay her glory in the dust.

The profession of acting did not originate with the Hebrews. It is not a part of the divine pattern. The Bible mentions it, but never approves it. Drama, as it has come down to us, had its rise in Greece. It was originally a part of the worship of the god Dionysus and was carried on with drunken revelry.

The Miracle Plays of medieval times have been brought forward to justify the modern religious movie. That is an unfortunate weapon to choose for the defense of the movie, for it will surely harm the man who uses it more than any argument I could think of just offhand.

The Miracle Plays had their big run in the Middle Ages. They were dramatic performances with religious themes staged for the entertainment of the populace. At their best they were misguided efforts to teach spiritual truths by dramatic representation; at their worst they were shockingly irreverent and thoroughly reprehensible. In some of them the Eternal God was portrayed as an old man dressed in white with a gilt wig! To furnish low comedy, the devil himself was introduced on the stage and allowed to cavort for the amusement of the spectators. Bible themes were used, as in the modern movie, but this did not save the whole thing from becoming so corrupt that the Roman Church had finally to prohibit its priests from having any further part in it.

Those who would appeal for precedent to the Miracle Plays have certainly overlooked some important facts. For instance, the vogue of the Miracle Play coincided exactly with the most dismally corrupt period the Church has ever known. When the Church emerged at last from its long moral night these plays lost popularity and finally passed away. And be it remembered, the instrument God used to bring the Church out of the darkness was not drama; it was the biblical one of Spirit-baptized preaching. Serious-minded men thundered the truth and the people turned to God.

Indeed, history will show that no spiritual advance, no revival, no upsurge of spiritual life has ever been associated with acting in any form. The Holy Spirit never honors pretense.

Can it be that the historic pattern is being repeated? That the appearance of the religious movie is symptomatic of the low state of spiritual health we are in today? I fear so. Only the absence of the Holy Spirit from the pulpit and lack of true discernment on the part of professing Christians can account for the spread of religious drama among so-called evangelical churches. A Spirit-filled church could not tolerate it.

4. They Who Present the Gospel Movie Owe It to the Public to Give Biblical Authority for Their Act: And This They Have Not Done.

The Church, as long as it is following the Lord, goes along in Bible ways and can give a scriptural reason for its conduct. Its members meet at stated times to pray together: This has biblical authority back of it. They gather to hear the Word of God expounded: this goes back in almost unbroken continuity to Moses. They sing psalms and hymns and spiritual songs: so they are commanded by the apostle. They visit the sick and relieve the sufferings of the poor: for this they have both precept and example in Holy Writ. They lay up their gifts and bring them at stated times to the church or chapel to be used in the Lord's work: this also follows the scriptural pattern. They teach and train and instruct; they appoint teachers and pastors and missionaries and send them out to do the work for which the Spirit has gifted them: all this has plain scriptural authority behind it. They baptize, then break bread and witness to the lost; they cling together through thick and thin; they bear each other's burdens and share each other's sorrows: this is as it should be, and for all this there is full authority.

Now, for the religious movie where is the authority? For such a serious departure from the ancient pattern, where is the authority? For introducing into the Church the pagan art of acting, where is the authority? Let the movie advocates quote just one verse, from any book of the Bible, in any translation, to justify its use. This they cannot do. The best they can do is to appeal to the world's psychology or repeat brightly that "modern times call for modern methods." But the Scriptures--quote from them one verse to authorize movie acting as an instrument of the Holy Ghost. This they cannot do.

Every sincere Christian must find scriptural authority for the religious movie or reject it, and every producer of such movies, if he would square himself before the faces of honest and reverent men, must either show scriptural credentials or go out of business.

But, says someone, there is nothing unscriptural about the religious movie; it is merely a new medium for the utterance of the old message, as printing is a newer and better method of writing and the radio an amplification of familiar human speech.

To this I reply: The movie is not the modernization or improvement of any scriptural method; rather it is a medium in itself wholly foreign to the Bible and altogether unauthorized therein. It is play acting---just that, and nothing more. It is the introduction into the work of God of that which is not neutral, but entirely bad. The printing press is neutral; so is the radio; so is the camera. They may be used for good or bad purposes at the will of the user. But play acting is bad in its essence in that it involves the simulation of emotions not actually felt. It embodies a gross moral contradiction in that it calls a lie to the service of truth.

Arguments for the religious movie are sometimes clever and always shallow, but there is never any real attempt to cite scriptural authority. Anything that can be said for the movie can be said also for aesthetic dancing, which is a highly touted medium for teaching religious truth by appeal to the eye. Its advocates grow eloquent in its praise--but where is it indicated in the blueprint?

5. God has ordained four methods only by which Truth shall prevail---and the religious movie is not one of them.

Without attempting to arrange these methods in order of importance, they are (1) prayer, (2) song, (3) proclamation of the message by means of words, and (4) good works. These are the four main methods which God has blessed. All other biblical methods are subdivisions of these and stay within their framework.

Notice these in order:

(1) Spirit-burdened prayer. This has been through the centuries a powerful agent for the spread of saving truth among men. A praying Church carried the message of the cross to the whole known world within two centuries after the coming of the Holy Spirit at Pentecost. Read the book of Acts and see what prayer has done and can do when it is made in true faith.

(2) Spirit-inspired song has been another mighty instrument in the spread of the Word among mankind. When the Church sings in the Spirit she draws men unto Christ. Where her song has been ecstatic expression of resurrection joy, it has acted wonderfully to prepare hearts for the saving message. This has no reference to professional

religious singers, expensive choirs nor the popular "gospel" chorus. These for the time we leave out of consideration. But I think no one will deny that the sound of a Christian hymn sung by sincere and humble persons can have a tremendous and permanent effect for good. The Welsh revival is a fair modern example of this.

(3) In the Old Testament, as well as in the New, when God would impart His mind to men He embodied it in a message and sent men out to proclaim it. This was done by means of speaking and writing on the part of the messenger. It was received by hearing and reading on the part of those to whom it was sent. We are all familiar with the verse, "Speak ye comfortably to Jerusalem, and cry unto her" (Isaiah 40:2). John the Baptist was called "The voice of one crying in the wilderness" (Matthew 3:3). Again we have, "And I heard a voice from heaven saying unto me, Write" (Revelation 14:13). And the Apostle John opens his great work called the Revelation by pronouncing a blessing upon him that readeth and them that bear and keep the words of the prophecy and the things which are written therein. The two words "proclaim" and "publish" sum up God's will as it touches His Word. In the Bible, men for the most part wrote what had been spoken; in our time men are commissioned to speak what has been written. In

both cases the agent is a word, never a picture, a dance or a pageant.

(4) By His healing deeds our Lord opened the way for His saving Words. He went about doing good, and His Church is commanded to do the same. Faber understood this when he wrote:

"And preach thee too, as love knows how

By kindly deeds and virtuous life."

Church history is replete with instances of missionaries and teachers who prepared the way for their message with deeds of mercy shown to men and women who were at first hostile but who melted under the warm rays of practical kindnesses shown to them in time of need. If anyone should object to calling good works a method, I would not argue the point. Perhaps it would be more accurate to say that they are an overflow into everyday life of the reality of what is being proclaimed.

These are God's appointed methods, set forth in the Bible and confirmed in centuries of practical application. The intrusion of other methods is unscriptural, unwarranted and in violation of spiritual laws as old as the world.

The whole preach-the-gospel-with-movies idea is founded upon the same basic assumptions as modernism--namely, that the Word of God is not final, and that we of this day have a perfect right to add to it or alter it wherever we think we can improve it.

A brazen example of this attitude came to my attention recently. Preliminary printed matter has been sent out announcing that a new organization is in process of being formed. It is to be called the "International Radio and Screen Artists Guild," and one of its two major objectives is to promote the movie as a medium for the spread of the gospel. Its sponsors, apparently, are not Modernists, but confessed Fundamentalists. Some of its declared purposes are: to produce movies "with or without a Christian slant"; to raise and maintain higher standards in the movie field (this would be done, it says here, by having "much prayer" with leaders of the movie industry); to "challenge people, especially young people, to those fields as they are challenged to go to foreign fields."

This last point should not be allowed to pass without some of us doing a little challenging on our own account. Does this new organization actually propose in seriousness to add another gift to the gifts of the Spirit listed in the New

Testament? To the number of the Spirit's gifts, such as pastor, teacher, evangelist, is there now to be added another, the gift of the movie actor? To the appeal for consecrated Christian young people to serve as missionaries on the foreign field is there to be added an appeal for young people to serve as movie actors? That is exactly what this new organization does propose in cold type over the signature of its temporary chairman. Instead of the Holy Spirit saying, "Separate me Barnabas and Saul for the work whereunto I have called them" (Acts 13:2), these people will make use of what they call a "Christian talent listing," to consist of the names of "Christian" actors who have received the Spirit's gift to be used in making religious movies.

Thus the order set up in the New Testament is openly violated, and by professed lovers of the gospel who say unto Jesus, "Lord, Lord," but openly set aside His Lordship whenever they desire. No amount of smooth talk can explain away this serious act of insubordination.

Saul lost a kingdom when he "forced" himself and took profane liberties with the priesthood. Let these movie preachers look to their crown. They may find themselves on the road to Endor some dark night soon.

6. The religious movie is out of harmony with the whole spirit of the Scriptures and contrary to the mood of true godliness.

To harmonize the spirit of the religious movie with the spirit of the Sacred Scriptures is impossible. Any comparison is grotesque and, if it were not so serious, would be downright funny. To imagine Elijah appearing before Ahab with a roll of film! Imagine Peter standing up at Pentecost and saying, "Let's have the lights out, please." When Jeremiah hesitated to prophesy, on the plea that he was not a fluent speaker, God touched his mouth and said, "I have put my words in thy mouth." Perhaps Jeremiah could have gotten on well enough without the divine touch if he had had a good 16mm projector and a reel of home-talent film.

Let a man dare to compare his religious movie show with the spirit of the Book of Acts. Let him try to find a place for it in the twelfth chapter of First Corinthians. Let him set it beside Savonarola's passionate preaching or Luther's thundering or Wesley's heavenly sermons or Edwards' awful appeals. If he cannot see the difference in kind, then he is too blind to be trusted with leadership in the Church of the Living God. The only thing that he can do appropriate to the circumstances is to drop to his knees and cry with poor Bartimaeus, "Lord, that I might receive my sight."

But some say, "We do not propose to displace the regular method of preaching the gospel. We only want to supplement it." To this I answer: If the movie is needed to supplement anointed preaching it can only be because God's appointed method is inadequate and the movie can do something which God's appointed method cannot do. What is that thing? We freely grant that the movie can produce effects which preaching cannot produce (and which it should never try to produce), but dare we strive for such effects in the light of God's revealed will and in the face of the judgment and a long eternity?

7. I AM AGAINST THE RELIGIOUS MOVIE BECAUSE OF THE HARMFUL EFFECT UPON EVERYONE ASSOCIATED WITH IT.

First, the evil effect upon the "actors" who play the part of the various characters in the show; this is not the less because it is unsuspected. Who can, while in a state of fellowship with God, dare to play at being a prophet? Who has the gall to pretend to be an apostle, even in a show? Where is his reverence? Where is his fear? Where is his humility? Any one who can bring himself to act a part for any purpose, must first have grieved the Spirit and silenced His voice within the heart. Then the whole business will appear good to him. "He feedeth on ashes; a deceived heart has turned him aside" (Isaiah 44:20). But he cannot escape the secret working of the ancient laws of the soul. Something high and fine and grand will die within him; and worst of all he will never suspect it. That is the curse that follows self-injury always. The Pharisees were examples of this. They were walking dead men, and they never dreamed how dead they were.

Secondly, it identifies religion with the theatrical world. I have seen recently in a fundamentalist magazine an advertisement of a religious film which would be altogether at home on the theatrical page on any city newspaper. Illustrated with the usual sex-bate picture of a young man and young woman in tender embrace, and spangled with such words as "feature-length, drama, pathos, romance," it reeked of Hollywood and the cheap movie house. By such business we are selling out our Christian separation, and nothing but grief can come of it late or soon.

Thirdly, the taste for drama which these pictures develop in the minds of the young will not long remain satisfied with the inferior stuff the religious movie can offer. Our young people will demand the real thing; and what can we reply when they ask why they should not patronize the regular movie house?

Fourthly, the rising generation will naturally come to look upon religion as another, and inferior, form of amusement. In fact, the present generation Yahwist has done this to an alarming extent already, and the gospel movie feeds the notion by fusing religion and fun in the name of orthodoxy. It takes no great insight to see that the religious movie must become increasingly more thrilling as the tastes of the spectators become more and more stimulated.

Fifthly, the religious movie is the lazy preacher's friend. If the present vogue continues to spread it will not be long before any man with enough ability to make an audible prayer, and mentality enough to focus a projector, will be able to pass for a prophet of the Most High God. The man of God can play around all week long and come up to the Lord's Day without a care. Everything has been done for him at the studio. He has only to set up the screen and lower the lights, and the rest follows painlessly.

Wherever the movie is used the prophet is displaced by the projector. The least that such displaced prophets can do is to admit that they are technicians and not preachers. Let them admit that they are not God-sent men, ordained of God for a sacred work. Let them put away their pretense.

Allowing that there may be some who have been truly called and gifted of God but who have allowed themselves to be taken in by this new plaything, the danger to such is still great. As long as they can fall back upon the movie, the pressure that makes preachers will be wanting. The habit and rhythm which belong to great preaching will be missing from their ministry. However great their natural gifts, however real their enduement of power, still they will never rise. They cannot while this broken reed lies close at hand to aid them in the crisis. The movie will doom them to be ordinary.

In Conclusion

One thing may bother some earnest souls: why so many good people approve the religious movie. The list of those who are enthusiastic about it includes many who cannot be written off as borderline Christians. If it is an evil, why have not these denounced it?

The answer is, lack of spiritual discernment. Many who are turning to the movie are the same who have, by direct teaching or by neglect, discredited the work of the Holy Spirit. They have apologized for the Spirit and so hedged Him in by their unbelief that it has amounted to an out-and-out repudiation. Now we are paying the price for our folly. The light has gone out and good men are forced to stumble around in the darkness of the human intellect.

The religious movie is at present undergoing a period of gestation and seems about to swarm over the churches like a cloud of locusts out of the earth. The figure is accurate; they are coming from below, not from above. The whole modern psychology has been prepared for this invasion of insects. The fundamentalists have become weary of manna and are longing for red flesh. What they are getting is a sorry substitute for the lusty and uninhibited pleasures of the world, but I suppose it is better than nothing, and it saves face by pretending to be spiritual.

Let us not for the sake of peace keep still while men without spiritual insight dictate the diet upon which God's children shall feed. I heard the president of a Christian college say some time ago that the Church is suffering from an "epidemic of amateurism." That remark is sadly true, and the religious movie represents amateurism gone wild. Unity among professing Christians is to be desired, but not at the expense of righteousness. It is good to go with the flock, but I for one refuse mutely to follow a misled flock over a precipice.

If God has given wisdom to see the error of religious shows we owe it to the Church to oppose them openly. We dare not take refuge in "guilty silence." Error is not silent; it is highly vocal and amazingly aggressive. We dare not be less so. But let us take heart: there are still many thousands of Christian people who grieve to see the world take over. If we draw the line and call attention to it we may be surprised how many people will come over on our side and help us drive from the Church this latest invader, the spirit of Hollywood.

ABOUT CROSSREACH PUBLICATIONS

Thank you for choosing CrossReach Publications.

Hope. Inspiration. Trust.

These three words sum up the philosophy of why CrossReach Publications exist. To create inspiration for the present thus inspiring hope for the future, through trusted authors from previous generations.

We are *non-denominational* and *non-sectarian.* We appreciate and respect what every part of the body brings to the table and believe everyone has the right to study and come to their own conclusions. We aim to help facilitate that end.

We aspire to excellence. If we have not met your standards please contact us and let us know. We want you to feel satisfied with your product. Something for everyone. We publish quality books both in presentation and content from a wide variety of authors who span various doctrinal positions and traditions, on a wide variety of Christian topics that will teach, encourage, challenge, inspire and equip.

We're a family-based home-business. A husband and wife team raising 8 kids. If you have any questions or comments about our publications email us at:

ContactUs@CrossReach.net

Don't forget you can follow us on Facebook and Twitter, (links are on the copyright page above) to keep up to date on our newest titles and deals.

BESTSELLING TITLES FROM CROSSREACH[1]

God Still Speaks
A. W. Tozer

Tozer is as popular today as when he was living on the earth. He is respected right across the spectrum of Christianity, in circles that would disagree sharply with him doctrinally. Why is this? A. W. Tozer was a man who knew the voice of God. He shared this experience with every true child of God. With all those who are called by the grace of God to share in the mystical union that is possible with Him through His Son Jesus.

Tozer fought against much dryness and formality in his day. Considered a mighty man of God by most Evangelicals today, he was unconventional in his approach to spirituality and had no qualms about consulting everyone from Catholic Saints to German Protestant mystics for inspiration on how to experience God more fully.

Tozer, just like his Master, doesn't fit neatly into our theological boxes. He was a man after God's own heart and was willing to break the rules (man-made ones that is) to get there.

---

[1] Buy from CrossReach Publications for quality and price. We have a full selection of titles in print and eBook. All available on the Amazon and Createspace stores. You can see our full selection just by searching for CrossReach Publications in the search bar!

Here are two writings by Tozer that touch on the heart of this goal. Revelation is Not Enough and The Speaking Voice. A bonus chapter The Menace of the Religious Movie is included.

This is meat to sink your spiritual teeth into. Tozer's writings will show you the way to satisfy your spiritual hunger.

What We Are In Christ

E. W. Kenyon

I was surprised to find that the expressions "in Christ," "in whom," and "in Him" occur more than 130 times in the New Testament. This is the heart of the Revelation of Redemption given to Paul.

Here is the secret of faith—faith that conquers, faith that moves mountains. Here is the secret of the Spirit's guiding us into all reality. The heart craves intimacy with the Lord Jesus and with the Father. This craving can now be satisfied.

Ephesians 1:7: "In whom we have our redemption through his blood, the remission of our trespasses according to the riches of his grace."

It is not a beggarly Redemption, but a real liberty in Christ that we have now. It is a Redemption by the God Who could say, "Let there be lights in the firmament of heaven," and cause the whole starry heavens to leap into being in a single instant. It is Omnipotence beyond human reason. This is where philosophy has never left a footprint.

Claiming Our Rights
E. W. Kenyon

There is no excuse for the spiritual weakness and poverty of the Family of God when the wealth of Grace and Love of our great Father with His power and wisdom are all at our disposal. We are not coming to the Father as a tramp coming to the door begging for food; we come as sons not only claiming our legal rights but claiming the natural rights of a child that is begotten in love. No one can hinder us or question our right of approach to our Father.

Satan has Legal Rights over the sinner that God cannot dispute or challenge. He can sell them as slaves; he owns them, body, soul and spirit. But the moment we are born again... receive Eternal Life, the nature of God,—his legal dominion ends.

Christ is the Legal Head of the New Creation, or Family of God, and all the Authority that was given Him, He has given us: (Matthew 28:18), "All authority in heaven," the seat of authority, and "on earth," the place of execution of authority. He is "head over all things," the highest authority in the Universe, for the benefit of the Church which is His body.

The Two Babylons
Alexander Hislop

Fully Illustrated High Res. Images. Complete and Unabridged.

Expanded Seventh Edition. This is the first and only seventh edition available in a modern digital edition. Nothing is left out! New material not found in the first six editions!!! Available in eBook and paperback edition exclusively from CrossReach Publications.

"In his work on "The Two Babylons" Dr. Hislop has proven conclusively that all the idolatrous systems of the nations had their origin in what was founded by that mighty Rebel, the beginning of whose kingdom was Babel (Gen. 10:10)."—A. W. Pink, The Antichrist (1923)

There is this great difference between the works of men and the works of God, that the same minute and searching investigation, which displays the defects and imperfections of the one, brings out also the beauties of the other. If the most finely polished needle on which the art of man has been expended be subjected to a microscope, many inequalities, much roughness and clumsiness, will be seen. But if the microscope be brought to bear on the flowers of the field, no such result appears. Instead of their beauty diminishing, new beauties and still more delicate, that have escaped the naked eye, are forthwith discovered; beauties that make us appreciate, in a way which otherwise we could have had little conception of, the full force of the Lord's saying, "Consider the lilies of the field, how they grow; they toil not, neither do they spin: and yet I say unto you, That even Solomon, in all his glory, was not arrayed like one of these." The same law appears also in comparing the Word of God and the most finished productions of men. There are spots and blemishes in the most admired productions of human genius. But the more the Scriptures are searched, the more minutely they are studied, the more their perfection appears; new beauties are brought into light every day; and the discoveries of science, the researches of the learned, and the labours of infidels, all alike conspire to illustrate the wonderful harmony of all the parts, and the Divine beauty that clothes the whole. If this be the case with Scripture in general, it is especially the case with prophetic Scripture. As every spoke in the wheel of Providence revolves, the prophetic symbols start into still more bold and beautiful relief. This is very strikingly the case with the prophetic language that forms the groundwork and corner-stone of the present work. There never has been any difficulty in the mind of any enlightened Protestant in identifying the woman "sitting on seven mountains," and having on her forehead the name written, "Mystery, Babylon the Great," with the Roman apostacy.

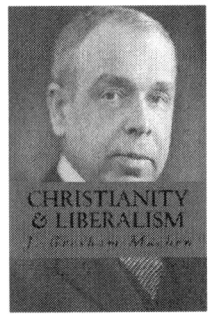

Christianity and Liberalism
J. Gresham Machen

The purpose of this book is not to decide the religious issue of the present day, but merely to present the issue as sharply and clearly as possible, in order that the reader may be aided in deciding it for himself. Presenting an issue sharply is indeed by no means a popular business at the present time; there are many who prefer to fight their intellectual battles in what Dr. Francis L. Patton has aptly called a "condition of low visibility." Clear-cut definition of terms in religious matters, bold facing of the logical implications of religious views, is by many persons regarded as an impious proceeding. May it not discourage contribution to mission boards? May it not hinder the progress of consolidation, and produce a poor showing in columns of Church statistics? But with such persons we cannot possibly bring ourselves to agree. Light may seem at times to be an impertinent intruder, but it is always beneficial in the end. The type of religion which rejoices in the pious sound of traditional phrases, regardless of their meanings, or shrinks from "controversial" matters, will never stand amid the shocks of life. In the sphere of religion, as in other spheres, the things about which men are agreed are apt to be the things that are least worth holding; the really important things are the things about which men will fight.

Elementary Geography
Charlotte Mason

This little book is confined to very simple "reading lessons upon the Form and Motions of the Earth, the Points of the Compass, the Meaning of a Map: Definitions."

It is hoped that these reading lessons may afford intelligent teaching, even in the hands of a young teacher.

Children should go through the book twice, and should, after the second reading, be able to answer any of the questions from memory.

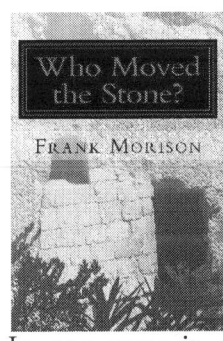

Who Moved the Stone?
Frank Morison

This study is in some ways so unusual and provocative that the writer thinks it desirable to state here very briefly how the book came to take its present form.

In one sense it could have taken no other, for it is essentially a confession, the inner story of a man who originally set out to write one kind of book and found himself compelled by the sheer force of circumstances to write another.

It is not that the facts themselves altered, for they are recorded imperishably in the monuments and in the pages of human history. But the interpretation to be put upon the facts underwent a change. Somehow the perspective shifted—not suddenly, as in a flash of insight or inspiration, but slowly, almost imperceptibly, by the very stubbornness of the facts themselves.

The book as it was originally planned was left high and dry, like those Thames barges when the great river goes out to meet the incoming sea. The writer discovered one day that not only could he no longer write the book as he had once conceived it, but that he would not if he could.

To tell the story of that change, and to give the reasons for it, is the main purpose of the following pages.

The Person and Work of the Holy Spirit
R. A. Torrey

Before one can correctly understand the work of the Holy Spirit, he must first of all know the Spirit Himself. A frequent source of error and fanaticism about the work of the Holy Spirit is the attempt to study and understand His work without first of all coming to know Him as a Person.

It is of the highest importance from the standpoint of worship that we decide whether the Holy Spirit is a Divine Person, worthy to receive our adoration, our faith, our love, and our entire surrender to Himself, or whether it is simply an influence emanating from God or a power or an illumination that God imparts to us. If the Holy Spirit is a person, and a Divine Person, and we do not know Him as such, then we are robbing a Divine Being of the worship and the faith and the love and the surrender to Himself which are His due.

How to Be Filled with the Holy Spirit
A. W. Tozer

Before we deal with the question of how to be filled with the Holy Spirit, there are some matters which first have to be settled. As believers you have to get them out of the way, and right here is where the difficulty arises. I have been afraid that my listeners might have gotten the idea somewhere that I had a how-to-be-filled-with-the-Spirit-in-five-easy-lessons doctrine, which I could give you. If you can have any such vague ideas as that, I can only stand before you and say, "I am sorry"; because it isn't true; I can't give you such a course. There are some things, I say, that you have to get out of the way, settled.

In His Steps
Charles M. Sheldon

The sermon story, In His Steps, or "What Would Jesus Do?" was first written in the winter of 1896, and read by the author, a chapter at a time, to his Sunday evening congregation in the Central

Congregational Church, Topeka, Kansas. It was then printed as a serial in The Advance (Chicago), and its reception by the readers of that paper was such that the publishers of The Advance made arrangements for its appearance in book form. It was their desire, in which the author heartily joined, that the story might reach as many readers as possible, hence succeeding editions of paper-covered volumes at a price within the reach of nearly all readers.

The story has been warmly and thoughtfully welcomed by Endeavor societies, temperance organizations, and Y. M. C. A.'s. It is the earnest prayer of the author that the book may go its way with a great blessing to the churches for the quickening of Christian discipleship, and the hastening of the Master's kingdom on earth.

Charles M. Sheldon.
Topeka, Kansas,
November, 1897.

WE OFFER A LARGE & GROWING SELECTION OF CHRISTIAN TITLES
ALL AVAILABLE ON AMAZON & OTHER ONLINE STORES
JUST SEARCH FOR CROSSREACH PUBLICATIONS!

Made in the USA
Middletown, DE
28 December 2018